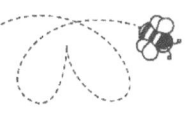

Beekeeping Adventures

An Introduction to Beginning a Step-by-Step Journey into the World of Bees

By Kay H. Theis

TABLE OF CONTENT

INTRODUCTION: 5

CHAPTER 1: THE ADVANTAGES OF BEEKEEPING 10

CHAPTER 2: REALISTIC EXPECTATIONS 13

CHAPTER 3: WHAT TOOLS ARE NEEDED TO GET STARTED?................16

CHAPTER 4: GETTING STARTED WITH BEEKEEPING............................47

CHAPTER 5: CHOOSING YOUR BEES...49

CHAPTER 7: BEEKEEPING SAFETY AND BEST PRACTICES....................54

CHAPTER 8: THE BEEHIVE'S LIFECYCLE 57

CHAPTER 9: BEEKEEPING TASKS THROUGHOUT THE YEAR..................60

CHAPTER 10: HARVESTING HONEY AND OTHER BEE PRODUCTS 63

CHAPTER 11 : EXPANDING YOUR BEEKEEPING KNOWLEDGE: 66

CHAPTER 12: TROUBLESHOOTING COMMON BEEKEEPING CHALLENGES..........69

CHAPTER 13: SUSTAINABLE BEEKEEPING PRACTICES 73

CONCLUSION: 77

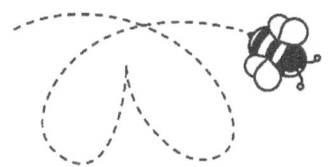

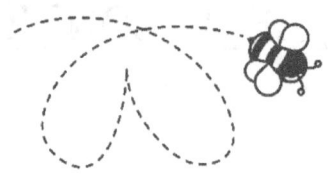

INTRODUCTION:

Beekeeping is a fun hobby that provides access to delectable Honey and supports the ecosystems in your neighbourhood. The benefits of beekeeping will be covered in his introduction, explaining why it is becoming increasingly popular among beginners.

Beekeeping promotes a unique and meaningful relationship with nature first and foremost. A vital custodian of bees, a beekeeper gains knowledge of bees' intricate social structure and helps ensure their survival. It is fantastic to observe the complex functions carried out within a beehive, to see the bees busy foraging and interacting, and to witness the wonder of honey production.

Another approach to protecting the environment is through beekeeping. There are several species of bees since they are necessary for pollinating plants. Bees must pollinate plants for many species, including many of the fruits, vegetables, and flowers that people depend on. You can grow bees by actively protecting biodiversity and halting the global decrease in bee populations.

Setting reasonable expectations is crucial for new beekeepers. Beekeeping needs perseverance, dedication, and ongoing learning. Honey should be collected, but first, it's essential to understand bee requirements, look after the hive's health, and give bees a healthy environment.

You will discover the fundamentals of this exciting sector in this book, along with the resources you need to launch a successful beekeeping venture. We'll guide you through the essentials, such as choosing the correct bees, putting up your hive, managing your colony throughout the seasons, and collecting Honey and other bee products, whether you have a little backyard or plenty of rural areas.

Prepare to explore the fascinating world of bees, take advantage of beekeeping's advantages, and help the environment. Let's get started on your fascinating beekeeping journey!

SECTION 1: WHY BEEKEEPING IS A FUN AND SUCCESSFUL HOBBY:

People from many areas of life are drawn to the exciting and gratifying beekeeping hobby. The following justifies why beekeeping is seen as a fun and fulfilling hobby:

SECTION 2: FASCINATING INSIGHT INTO NATURE:

Beekeeping offers a rare chance to see a beehive in operation and learn more about the fascinating world of bees. As a beekeeper, you can observe the complex hierarchy and labour division inside a hive. People are always amazed by bee behaviour, which ranges from meticulous foraging to difficult communication using dance-like gestures.

SECTION 3: RELATIONSHIP WITH THE NATURAL WORLD:

Beekeeping enables you to develop a strong bond with nature. As you look after your bees and see how they interact with the environment and plants, you'll better understand how ecosystems are interrelated. Your understanding of the interdependence of bees, plants, and other species deepens, enhancing your concern for the environment.

SECTION 4: THE SENSATION OF ACHIEVEMENT:

As you look after and care for your bee colonies, beekeeping makes you feel accomplished. You feel tremendous pride in your accomplishments as your hive develops and grows, the bees thrive under your care, and you enjoy the Honey and other fruits of your labours. Through beekeeping, you may actively support the health and vitality of a living creature.

Beekeeping promotes the growth of foods that are acquired locally and sustainably. Bees may aid in agricultural pollination and boost the output of fruits, vegetables, and nuts. This practical involvement in food production promotes a deeper comprehension of the origin and standard of our food. Beekeeping has several rewarding elements, including the ability to harvest Honey, a healthy and natural sweetener.

Beekeeping is a hobby that offers many opportunities for lifelong learning and growth. There is still much to learn about bees, hive management strategies, honey production, and apiculture. Beekeeping encourages ongoing education, workshops, and networking with other beekeepers, all promoting personal development and knowledge advancement.

SECTION 5: CONTRIBUTION TO CONSERVATION EFFORTS:

Actively raising bees helps protect biodiversity and pollinators. Bee populations face a variety of challenges across the world, including disease, pesticide exposure, and habitat deterioration. As a beekeeper, you support the preservation of healthy ecosystems by protecting these essential pollinators, providing habitat for bees, and raising awareness of their importance.

Beekeeping is a fulfilling pastime that provides chances for lifelong learning, a solid connection to nature, and a feeling of success. You can participate in programs supporting environmental preservation, sustainable food production, and individual growth. Whether you are passionate about sustainable agriculture or the natural world, beekeeping provides a gratifying and informative experience.

CHAPTER 1: THE ADVANTAGES OF BEEKEEPING

SECTION 1: THE ADVANTAGES OF BEEKEEPING FOR LOCAL ECOSYSTEMS AND THE ENVIRONMENT

Beekeeping is crucial for promoting biodiversity and maintaining the health of local ecosystems since it has numerous positive impacts on the environment and ecosystems in a given location. Here are some notable benefits of beekeeping:

Bees are beautiful pollinators that assist plants in reproducing and producing fruits, vegetables, and seeds by carrying pollen from male to female flower parts. Nearly 80% of flowering plants rely on pollinators like bees for successful reproduction. By keeping bees, you may actively encourage pollination, which supports the growth of crops, wildflowers, and trees. As a result, the region's biodiversity is enhanced, and additional species may reach food sources.

SECTION 2: HABITAT CONSERVATION:

Keeping bees can help with habitat preservation. Creating adequate bee habitats is essential as natural habitats disappear due to urbanization and land-use changes. Beekeepers frequently make bee nesting areas, native floral plants, and pollinator-friendly landscapes. With the help of these projects, bees and other beneficial insects now have oases of habitat to call home in both urban and agricultural settings.

SECTION 3: GENETIC DIVERSITY:

Beekeeping helps to maintain the genetic variety of bees. To remain resilient and adaptive in the face of diseases, pests, and habitat loss, honeybee populations must be kept diverse. Working with certain bee breeds and strains, beekeepers deliberately select bees for desirable characteristics like illness resistance, productivity, and obedience. Beekeepers preserve genetic diversity among honeybee populations through prudent breeding and management techniques.

SECTION 4: ENVIRONMENTAL EDUCATION:

Beekeeping offers a fantastic platform for environmental awareness and education. Individuals are becoming more aware of the interdependence of bees, plants, and ecosystems as more individuals raise bees. By letting others know about this information, you increase awareness of the value of pollinators, the necessity of conservation efforts, and the associated difficulties. Beekeepers are actively involved in public education campaigns highlighting bees' importance in maintaining ecological balance. These activities may include making lectures, hosting seminars, or visiting events.

SECTION 5: HONEY PRODUCTION:

While beekeeping has many positive effects on the environment, it's also vital to highlight the mouthwatering benefit that comes with it: honey production. Honey is a natural sweetener that beekeepers may gather and utilize in various culinary applications. Beekeepers support sustainable agriculture by sourcing their Honey locally and advocating the consumption of minimally processed, locally sourced foods.

Beekeeping is essential for preserving the environment and regional ecosystems overall. By becoming a beekeeper, you may actively contribute to pollination, habitat protection, genetic variety preservation, environmental education, and sustainable honey production, which will benefit the environment and the welfare of both human and animal groups.

CHAPTER 2: REALISTIC EXPECTATIONS

SECTION 1: SETTING REALISTIC EXPECTATIONS AS A BEGINNER BEEKEEPER:

A successful and pleasurable experience as a new beekeeper depends on having reasonable expectations. For you to begin beekeeping with the proper mentality, it's critical to comprehend the following elements:

SECTION 2: LEARNING CURVE:

To become a master beekeeper, you must have both knowledge and experience. Understanding that there will be a gradual learning curve is essential. Even though you might encounter obstacles and setbacks, you can overcome them by exercising patience, perseverance, and a commitment to lifelong learning. Prepare to study best practices, hive upkeep, and bee biology.

Start Small: For novices, beginning with a few hives is advised. Managing many colonies may be time-consuming and challenging. Starting small with one or two packets will let you concentrate on learning the nuances of beekeeping without being overwhelmed. Your beekeeping operation could progressively grow as you acquire expertise and confidence.

SECTION 3: SEASONAL VARIATIONS:

Beekeeping is a seasonal occupation, and the demands placed on beekeepers change throughout the year. Be aware that the workload might vary depending on the season and that various management strategies are needed. For instance, the intensity of hive inspections, pest control, and honey harvest may increase throughout spring and summer. During the cooler months, the focus shifts to bee survival and preparations for the coming winter. Knowing these seasonal differences may create reasonable time commitments and effort expectations.

SECTION 4: HONEY PRODUCTION:

Although honey production is a fascinating component of beekeeping, it's essential to understand that it could be insignificant for the first year or two. Before producing excess Honey, bees need time to settle in and develop their colony. Prioritize your bee colonies' well-being and expansion as a novice instead of anticipating a significant honey yield.

SECTION 5: BEE HEALTH AND LOSSES:

To maintain your bees healthy, you must manage threats from illnesses, pests, and environmental elements. Losses can happen despite your best efforts. It is essential to realize that beekeeping involves occasional losses on occasion. If you prepare for future obstacles and failures, you will approach them with resilience and a problem-solving mentality.

SECTION 6: PERSONAL INTERACTIONS:

Some individuals find interacting with bees intimidating, which is required for beekeeping. Managing your assumptions of how each individual will react to bees is essential. As your confidence and competence grow, you'll feel more at ease working your bees. Your safety depends on wearing the appropriate protection gear, which may be altered to meet your comfort level throughout beekeeping activities.

As a novice beekeeper, you may approach the experience with a reasonable expectation level, patience, and an openness to learning. A successful and rewarding beekeeping experience will depend on knowing the learning curve, starting small, doing things slowly, taking into account seasonal differences, being patient with honey production, predicting problems with bee health, and regulating personal comfort levels.

CHAPTER 3: WHAT TOOLS ARE NEEDED TO GET STARTED?

These are the basic beekeeping supplies and tools you will require. As your beekeeping business expands and you gain more expertise, you could need additional tools and specialized equipment.

These are:

1. Beehive

2. Beekeeping Suit or Protective Clothing

3. Smoker

4. Hive Tool

5. Bee Brush

6. Uncapping Knife or Fork

7. Honey Extractor

8. Feeder

9. Beekeeping Journal or Notebook

10. First Aid Kit

1. Beehive:

Honeybees reside and construct their comb mostly in beehives. Their residence gives the bees a secure and orderly setting to do their daily business. Below is a detailed explanation of the components and characteristics of a typical beehive:

A beehive is made up of one or more boxes or supers piled on top of one another. The bees use these rectangular chambers to nurture brood (emerging bees), store honey, and construct their comb. The size and power of the bee colony will determine how many containers are needed.

Frames: Vertically hung structures are placed within each box. The shelves—which might be made of wood or plastic—hold the beeswax comb. They give the bees a well-organized foundation to build their comb and make it possible for beekeepers to remove and examine the frames during hive maintenance rapidly.

Foundation: A foundation is a sheet of plastic or beeswax positioned inside the frame. It gives the bees a foundation on which to construct their comb. Depending on whether the structure is being used for honey or brood storage, the foundation can be profound, medium, or shallow in size.

Inner Cover: The uppermost box is topped with a board known as the inner cover, which acts as the hive's insulation and ventilation system. It often features a central hole or notch that the bees use as an entrance and exit. The inner cover controls the airflow and temperature inside the hive.

Outer Cover: The beehive's highest part is the outer cover. It shields against weather hazards, including rain and chilly temperatures. The outer shell, made of wood or other durable materials, protects and keeps the hive dry.

Bottom Board: The bees' entrance is on the bottom board, which acts as the beehive's foundation. It gives the hive security and support. The ventilation and access to the hive may be managed by beekeepers thanks to specific bottom panels' movable openings.

Hive Stand: The hive is raised off the ground by a hive stand construction. The chance of water damage is decreased, and it aids in protecting the pack from moisture and pests. The hive stand may be a straightforward wooden platform or a custom-made frame.

Beehives are frequently painted or polished to keep the wood from deteriorating and increase longevity. Non-toxic paint or finishes are commonly used to protect bees. Depending on the region, the colour of the hive can also aid in heat absorption or reflectance.

Depending on the hive type, such as Langstroth, top bar, or Warre hives, beehives can be built in various ways. The overall goal of creating good honeybee homes stays the same, although each hive type has distinctive qualities.

Beehives are purposefully created to closely resemble the natural habitat of bees and enable beekeepers to manage and extract Honey with the most minor damage to the colony. They ensure the well-being and production of the area by giving the bees a safe and orderly place to perform their fundamental tasks.

2. Beekeeping Suit or Protective Clothing:

Beekeepers must wear beekeeping suits or other protective clothing to ensure their security and safety while doing hive inspections and other beekeeping chores. They reduce the possibility of stings by serving as a physical barrier between the beekeeper and the bees. Detailed information about beekeeping attire and protective equipment is provided below:

Full-Body costume: A typical beekeeping costume covers the wearer's whole body from head to toe. A lightweight, breathable fabric that protects bees' stings is used to make the case. Since light colours are less attractive to bees, the claim often needs to be stronger in colour.

Veil or Helmet: A cover or helmet worn over the beekeeper's head and face while they are dressed in the suit protects their head and neck from bee stings. The veil is typically constructed of a thin mesh material that provides decent visibility while keeping bees away from the face and neck region.

Gloves: Gloves made specifically for beekeeping are a crucial component of safety gear. For protection against bee stings, they are made to cover the hands and wrists. A robust, sting-resistant material, such as leather, is often used to make the gloves. Some gloves come with extended gauntlets that reach up the forearm for additional protection.

Boots and Socks: Beekeepers frequently don long boots that conceal their lower legs and ankles. The shoes shield the wearer from bee stings and allow them to tuck their jeans inside the boots to discourage bees from climbing up their legs. To give another layer of protection between the skin and the shoes, it is advised to wear thick socks.

Elastic cuffs at the wrists and ankle straps are possible accessories for beekeeping outfits to provide a tight and secure fit. This guarantees that the suit stays in place throughout beekeeping tasks and helps prevent bees from getting inside the case through any holes.

Breathability and Ventilation: To guarantee comfort during prolonged usage, beekeeping outfits and protective equipment are made to be breathable. They frequently have mesh inserts or ventilation panels in sweat-prone regions like the back and armpits to promote airflow and minimize overheating.

Suit Maintenance: To preserve the efficiency of beekeeping suits and protective clothes, frequent inspection and upkeep are required. Tears, holes, and worn-out case areas should be inspected for bee entrance places. The integrity and lifespan of the protective clothes are preserved by routine washing and careful storage.

Beekeepers must wear beekeeping suits and other protective clothes to protect themselves from bee stings when working with bees. By putting on a well-fitting and kept-up case, beekeepers may comfortably carry out hive inspections and other tasks. This ensures their safety and frees them up to concentrate more on the health of the bees.

3. Smoker:

Honeybees must be calmed during hive inspections and operations requiring a smoker. By interfering with the bees' communication system, the cold smoke it creates suppresses their protective behaviour. Here is a thorough explanation of a smoker:

Construction: Typically, a smoker comprises a metal chamber, bellows, and nozzle or spout. The canister is frequently made out of stainless steel or galvanized metal to withstand the heat created by the burning chemical. It features a hinged cover or aperture, making the fuel chamber easily accessible.

Fuel Chamber: The lowest portion of the smoker is called the fuel chamber, where combustible materials are burned to generate smoke. Beekeepers use a wide variety of materials as fuel, including but not restricted to:

Smoker Fuel: Common fuels for smokers include compressed cotton, burlap, straw, dried wood chips, pine needles, twigs, and dried pine needles. These substances produce cool, thick smoke without leaving hazardous or poisonous residues behind.

Bellows: The smoker's top-mounted bellows deliver a steady stream of air to keep the fuel burning. A handle that swings back and forth to create airflow and force air into the fuel chamber is commonly used to operate it.

Nozzle or Spout: The smoke is directed toward the beehive via the nozzle or spout that protrudes from the canister. When inspecting hives, it enables the beekeeper to manage the direction and strength of the smoke.

How it Works: The beekeeper begins by igniting the fuel in the chamber before using the smoker. Once ignited, the fire is maintained by pumping air through the bellows to keep it smoking. The beekeeper then directs the smoke toward the beehive's entrance and other bee-inhabited places.

Effects on Bees: The introduction of smoke into the beehive prompts a defensive reaction from the bees. They automatically leave the hive because they suspect a forest fire may be starting. Honey is consumed as a result, which reduces the likelihood of bee stings. The smoke also obscures the guard bees' pheromones, preventing them from communicating and curbing their aggressive behaviour.

Safety Considerations: To avoid fires or injury to the bees, it is crucial to use caution while utilizing a smoker. The smoker must be used with appropriate airflow on a fireproof surface. Additionally, beekeepers should ensure it is properly extinguished and cold before storing or moving the smoker.

Beekeepers may deal with honeybees more successfully and securely thanks to smokers, valuable instruments in the beekeeping trade. Beekeepers can reduce the danger of stings and disruptions and enable easier hive inspections and operations by employing cold smoke to quiet the bees.

4. Hive Tool:

A hive tool is a multipurpose and essential beekeeping instrument used for various operations requiring the management of beehives. It's designed to simplify for beekeepers to pry apart hive components, remove wax and propolis, and perform other essential hive maintenance duties. A hive tool is described in full below:

Construction: A hive tool generally consists of a handle and a flat, solid metal blade with a hooked or curled end. Hardened steel or sturdy, rust-resistant stainless steel makes the blade. The handle, which might be constructed of wood, plastic, or metal, gives the beekeeper a secure hold.

Blade and Hook: Its blade is the flat, tapered section that protrudes from the handle of the hive tool. The beekeeper may pry apart hive parts like frames, boxes, and supers with this tool since it fits into tiny openings and crevices inside the hive. For cutting or scraping activities, the blade may have a sharp edge.

The opposite end of the hive tool has a hooked lot embedded in the curved part of the blade. It is used to break apart firmly bonded wax or propolis, remove frames from the hive, and separate buildings.

How to Use a Hive Tool:

Hives opening To open beehives, a hive tool is required. It enables beekeepers to separate and lift hive parts like hive boxes or supers that could otherwise be bound together by beeswax or propolis.

Frame Manipulation: For inspections, honey extraction, or other operations, hive tools raise and remove frames from the hive. The tool's hooked end can be used to aid in separating securely fastened edges of the pack.

Scraping and Cleaning: The hive tool's flat blade scrapes extra propolis, beeswax, or other detritus off hive components. It aids in keeping the hive clean and tidy, enabling better bee management and lowering the risk of illnesses or pests.

Queen Examinations: During queen inspections, the hive tool may deftly lift or manipulate frames. It enables beekeepers to find and watch the queen without endangering them or the bees.

Safety considerations: To avoid damage, using hive tools cautiously is essential. Beekeepers should use caution while pulling or handling hive components since the blade and hooked end can be sharp. This will help to prevent harm to the hive or the bees. To stop infections from spreading between packs, frequently cleaning and sterilizing the hive tool is also advised.

The hive tool is crucial to beekeeping because it gives beekeepers the leverage and accuracy they need to carry out numerous hive management chores. It is a valuable tool for beekeepers of all levels of expertise, assisting in the appropriate administration and maintenance of honeybee colonies thanks to its adaptability and practical design.

5. Bee Brush:

The delicate removal of bees from hive parts or frames without endangering them requires the use of a bee brush, a specialist equipment. It is intended to assist beekeepers in controlling bees while doing hive inspections, collecting Honey, or performing other operations that call for the temporary removal of bees. Here is a thorough explanation of the bee brush:

Construction: A bee brush generally has a handle and flexible, supple bristles. The bristles are made from horsehair, other natural materials, or synthetic fibres that are favourable to bees. The handle is ergonomically built for a secure grasp and is frequently constructed of wood or plastic.

Bristles: A bee brush has soft, bendable bristles to prevent hurting the bees. They are tightly packed to brush the bees without harming or crushing them efficiently. Because the strands are frequently bright in colour, beekeepers can more easily distinguish the bees against the backdrop.

Uses of a Bee Brush:

Bee brushes are frequently used to sweep bees off frames during hive inspections gently. Beekeepers may monitor the buildings and carry out a variety of operations, including checking for brood, diagnosing diseases, and putting or removing honey supers.

Harvesting Honey: Using bee brushes can help in honey extraction. They can be used to remove bees from honeycomb cells so that there are fewer bees around when Honey is extracted, and the cap is removed. This lessens the possibility of bees becoming caught or hurt during the extraction of Honey.

Collecting Swarms: Swarms gathered on objects or surfaces can occasionally be removed with bee brushes. By gently brushing the bees into a collecting container or hive, beekeepers may safely catch and move the swarm.

Queen Bee Management: Bees may be moved using bee brushes during queen raising or replacement operations. Beekeepers can change the queen's location within the hive by gently stroking her from one region to another.

Proper Usage: Using a bee brush properly and gently is imperative to prevent hurting the bees. Beekeepers should use gentle, sweeping strokes instead of using undue power to push the bees away. To avoid harm, it's best to avoid the bee's abdomen or wings directly.

Cleaning and Maintenance: To preserve cleanliness and stop the spread of illnesses or pests, bee brushes should be washed and sanitized often. It is usually sufficient to wash and thoroughly rinse the brushes in warm, soapy water. Beekeepers should also look for signs of wear or damage on the bee brush and make any necessary repairs.

With bee brushes, beekeepers may control bees without endangering or stressing the colony. Beekeepers can complete necessary chores while preserving the general health and well-being of the hive by gently brushing bees away from frames or other hive components.

6. Uncapping Knife or Fork:

An uncapping knife or fork is a specialized instrument used in beekeeping to remove beeswax cappings from honeycomb frames. It is a crucial instrument for beekeepers to access Honey and prepare it for extraction during the honey extraction process. The proper procedure for removing the caps from knives and forks is detailed below:

Uncapping Knife:

Construction: Stainless steel or another heat-resistant material often makes up an uncapping knife's long, thin blade. Typically, the edge has serrations on either one or both sides, which makes it easier to cut through beeswax cappings efficiently. The knife handle is composed of wood, plastic, or metal and is shaped for a secure grip.

Blade Styles: Straight and wavy/serrated blades are two of the many available uncapping knives. Straight blades deliver a smooth, accurate cut, whereas wavy or jagged edges make it easier to shatter the cappings.

Heat Source: Some uncapping knives have electrical heating elements, which warm up the blade for simpler and smoother uncapping. Large-scale honey extraction operations can benefit from the use of these electric knives.

Usage: An uncapping knife gently glides the heated blade or serrated edge down the honeycomb frame's surface to cut through the beeswax cappings. The cappings are removed while causing the least harm to the comb possible by carefully moving the knife.

Uncapping Fork:

An uncapping fork, often called an uncapping scratcher, is made of a handle and tines or prongs. The tips of the tines are generally sharp, pointed stainless steel.

Use: To use an uncapping fork, softly run the sharp tines over the surface of a honeycomb frame covered in beeswax. This will pierce and lift the beeswax cappings. As a result, the Honey is exposed for extraction.

Fork vs Knife: Small-scale or hobby beekeeping operations, where a lesser volume of Honey is harvested, often employ uncapping instruments. They offer good results for infrequent usage and are a more affordable option than uncapping knives.

Uncapping Process:

The thin coating of beeswax cappings that seal the honey-filled cells in the honeycomb frame are removed with uncapping knives and forks. The Honey is exposed and may be collected more readily by removing these cappings.

Uncapping forks are often used to pull or scrape over the cappings, while uncapping knives typically slice along the honeycomb frame's surface.

The uncapping procedure calls for accuracy and caution to prevent harm or severe disruption to the honeycomb. All cappings must be removed uniformly to allow the Honey to flow out during extraction.

Cleaning and Maintenance: After usage, beeswax residue should be removed entirely from uncapping knives and forks. They may be soaked in warm, soapy water or cleaned with a specialized beeswax cleaning solution. All beeswax must be removed to stop illnesses or pests from spreading between honeycombs.

Uncapping knives and forks are valuable for extracting Honey because they let beekeepers quickly and effectively remove beeswax cappings from honeycomb frames rapidly and effectively. Beekeepers may ensure a clean and easy extraction procedure that produces high-quality Honey by utilizing these instruments properly.

7. Honey Extractor:

In beekeeping, a honey extractor is used to separate Honey from the frames of the honeycomb without damaging or degrading the comb. Beekeepers can effectively remove Honey from their hives while maintaining the comb's integrity so that the bees can reuse it. Here is a thorough explanation of honey extractors:

A honey extractor's primary components are a drum or container, a frame holding or basket, a central spindle, and a crank or motorized device to rotate it. The drum or container is intended to hold the honeycomb frames during extraction and is often made of sturdy plastic or food-grade stainless steel.

Types of Honey Extractors:

Extractors that must be operated manually involve the beekeeper rotating the frames using a hand crank. Manual extractors are appropriate for small-scale beekeeping operations or beekeepers with fewer hives.

Motorized Extractors: These extractors use an electric motor to rotate the frames automatically. Motorized extractors are better for larger-scale beekeeping operations or beekeepers with more massive colonies since they save time and are more effective.

Usage: The following stages are taken throughout the honey extraction process:

Uncapping: The beekeeper uses an uncapping knife or fork to remove the beeswax cappings from the honeycomb cells, revealing the Honey, before inserting the frames in the honey extractor.

Frames are inserted into the holder or basket within the honey extractor while uncapped. To enable the best honey extraction, the structures are arranged radially.

Rotation: After loading the frames, the motorized mechanism is started, or the centre spindle is manually engaged. Centrifugal force is used by the rotating edges within the honey extractor to separate the Honey from the comb.

Honey collection: The Honey is ejected from the comb cells as the frames spin and gathers at the bottom of the drum or container. It then descends to the extractor's base, where a honey gate or valve can be used to control it.

Two Types of Honey Extraction:

Tangential Extraction: This technique removes just one side of the honeycomb frames. The edges are flipped to extract the Honey from the second side once the first side has been removed—shallow structures or frames with a wired base for enhanced stability work best for tangential extraction.

Radial Extraction: The honeycomb frames' two sides are concurrently removed in this technique. Radial extraction is appropriate for structures with deep comb cells or frames without wired foundations.

Cleaning and upkeep: After extraction, the honey extractor must be cleaned entirely to eliminate any leftover honey or debris. It is essential to keep things clean enough to prevent the spread of diseases or contamination during future extractions. Take the honey extractor apart, wash it in warm, soapy water, and rinse it well. It is essential to clean the extractor's crevices and moving parts thoroughly.

With honey extractors, beekeepers can effectively collect Honey while preserving the honeycomb for future use by the bees. Beekeepers may use honey extractors to harvest Honey, which disrupts the colony as little as possible and ensures the bees may continue producing Honey and constructing settlements.

8. Feeder:

In beekeeping, a feeder is a crucial instrument for supplementing the diet of honeybee colonies when their access to natural nectar sources is restricted or nonexistent. It aids in ensuring the bees have a sufficient food supply, particularly during absences or while establishing new colonies. Here is a thorough explanation of beekeeping feeders:

Purpose: The main goal of a feeder is to provide bees with other food to augment their natural foragings, such as sugar syrup or artificial pollen. Feeding is essential for preserving the colony's health and vigour, encouraging the rearing of the young, and assisting in the production of Honey.

Types of Feeders:

Boardman Feeder: A shallow tray or jar at the hive's entrance serves as this feeder. Bees may obtain the feed through tiny openings or slits without entering the hive. Beekeeping enterprises on a small scale can employ Boardman feeders since they are simple to use.

Top Feeder: Usually under the outer cover, a full feeder is a container placed atop the hive. Both the bees and the syrup may be easily accessed and retain more syrup. Top feeders frequently feature floats or screens to keep bees from drowning in the syrup.

Frame Feeder: Frame feeders are made to fit within the hive and replace one or more brood chamber frames. They provide the bees with direct access and are loaded with syrup or imitation pollen. Frame feeders are practical and reduce hive disruptions when feeding.

Entrance Feeder: An entry feeder is a container near the hive's entrance, much like the Boardman feeder. Bees may reach the feed from the front of the hive, but it might need extra protection from other bees robbing it.

Feeder Material: Feeders come in various materials, including glass, wood, and plastic. Plastic feeders are frequently used because of their sturdiness, cleaning simplicity, and dampness resistance. Beekeepers may visually check the feed level with glass feeders, although they are more delicate. Although less frequent, wooden feeders can be made to match particular hive arrangements.

Syrup Preparation: Sugar syrup is the most typical food for bees since it resembles the nectar they naturally collect from flowers. Granulated sugar is often dissolved in water at a precise ratio, such as 1:1 (equal parts sugar and water) or 2:1 (twice as much sugar as water), to create the syrup. The syrup should be heated while being constantly stirred to dissolve the sugar. Replacement feeders supply artificial pollen to meet the bees' additional protein needs.

Feeding Considerations:

Timing: Feeders are employed when establishing new colonies or during poor nectar flow. Feeding bees when natural food supplies are limited, or settlements require increased food production is essential.

Beehive Management: Beekeepers must monitor the feed levels and replenish the feeders as necessary. Keeping the feeders clear of dirt and mould that the bees may ingest is crucial.

Robbing Prevention: Beekeepers should exercise vigilance since other bees or wasps may steal their hives. With effective hive management, such as using entrance reducers or restricting hive openings, theft may be prevented.

Cleaning and Maintenance: To avoid the growth of mould, bacteria, or contaminants, feeders should be cleaned and sanitized often. They may be cleaned with warm, soapy water and washed adequately before refilling.

Feeders are crucial equipment that enables beekeepers to supply honeybee colonies with necessary food sources. Beekeepers may support the gadget if they use feeders properly and keep up robust hive management techniques.

9. Beekeeping Journal or Notebook:

A beekeeping diary or notebook is a valuable tool that beekeepers use to keep track of hive activity, record observations, and record important information about their beekeeping endeavours. Beekeepers can use it as a personal record-keeping system to track seasonal changes, keep track of their hives' development, and make decisions based on experience. Here is a thorough explanation of beekeeping diaries or notebooks:

Purpose:

Data Recording: A beekeeper's notebook allows them to keep track of vital information regarding their hives, such as hive inspections, colony health, honey production, queen status, observations of pests and diseases, and other pertinent information. It functions as a primary location for recording hive activity.

Analysis and Evaluation: Beekeepers can examine trends, patterns, and correlations in hive behaviour, honey output, or disease incidences by keeping a log. They can decide on effective hive management tactics and pinpoint problem areas using this information.

Historical Reference: A beekeeper's experiences and observations throughout time are documented in a journal. It may be a valuable tool for comparison and reference over many seasons or years, assisting beekeepers in spotting trends or changes in hive behaviour.

Content and Organization: Beekeepers can keep a record of the specifics of their hive inspections, including the date, the weather, the observations they made about the hive, the patterns of the brood, the amount of Honey on hand, and any interventions they made, such feeding or adding supers.

Swarm Activity: Beekeepers can successfully track and manage swarm prevention methods by noting any swarm cells or indicators of swarming they see during inspections.

Honey Production: The notebook can record when Honey was extracted, how much was taken, and which particular hives or frames the Honey came from. Beekeepers may use this information to evaluate the production of their hives and make future honey harvest plans.

Pest and Disease Management: Beekeepers can record any evidence of pests, illnesses, or anomalies found in the hive, as well as any supplemental interventions or treatments used.

Queen Performance: During inspections, beekeepers can note details about queens, including the introduction dates, health status, quantity, and quality of the brood. This aids in assessing the effectiveness and durability of queens.

Format and Accessibility:

Physical notebook: Some beekeepers like to keep a conventional notebook of paper and pen in which they handwrite their observations and comments. It is possible to utilize a specific notebook or diary with pre-formatted sections for various types of material.

Digital Journal: Technology has also led to the availability of digital beekeeping periodicals and software programs. These offer a practical approach to electronically collecting and storing data, enabling quick access, searchability, and data analysis. Digital diaries include several capabilities, including reminders, data graphing, and device syncing.

Benefits:

Documentation and analysis: By keeping a detailed and well-organized record of their actions, beekeepers can monitor their progress, spot patterns, and assess the effectiveness of their hives.

Decision-Making: When making management choices, putting ideas into practice, or resolving problems, the information kept in the diary is an invaluable resource.

Learning and Sharing: Beekeepers can take stock of their experiences, draw lessons from their triumphs and failures, and impart information to other beekeepers by keeping a diary. It may also be a teaching tool for beginners or aspiring beekeepers.

Tips:

Consistency: Form the routine of noting observations and updating the diary following each hive check or actual occurrence.

Accuracy and Detail: Include dates, proper hive names or numbers, and illustrative remarks in the logbook. Be as clear and thorough as possible.

Weather Conditions: Include details about the weather during hive inspections, as weather can significantly impact hive behaviour and productivity.

10. First Aid Kit:

Any beekeeper needs a first aid pack as part of their equipment. Because beekeeping includes interacting with bees, there is always a chance of getting stung or suffering from other minor wounds. In an emergency, a well-stocked first aid pack can assist beekeepers in providing immediate care and treatment. Here is a thorough explanation of first aid supplies for beekeepers:

Importance of a First Aid Kit:

Prompt Care: A first aid package enables beekeepers to treat minor wounds like bee stings, scratches, scrapes, or burns right away. It lessens the effects of injuries and stops them from getting worse.

Safety precautions: Beekeeping has certain inherent dangers, such as the possibility of allergic responses to bee stings or workplace accidents. A first aid kit guarantees the availability of the supplies required to manage these hazards and advance safety.

Emergency Preparedness: A first aid pack can give immediate care in case of more serious accidents or medical problems while you wait for expert assistance.

Essential Items in a Beekeeper's First Aid Kit:

AAdhesive Bandages: Abrasions, wounds, and blisters of various sizes can be treated using adhesive bandages (such as band-aids).

Dressings: Sterile gauze pads or dressings can cover more extensive wounds and speed up healing.

Antiseptic Solution: Antiseptic wipes or solutions to clean wounds reduce the risk of infection.

Bee Sting Relief: Supplies for treating bee stings, such as sting relief pads, antihistamine lotions or ointments, or ice packs to minimize pain and swelling, should be kept on hand by beekeepers.

Disposable gloves shield the wounded person and the beekeeper from contamination.

Tweezers: Tweezers can remove stingers or foreign objects from wounds.

Scissors: Scissors are handy for cutting dressings or tape.

Painkillers: You can add over-the-counter painkillers like acetaminophen or ibuprofen to get brief relief from pain or discomfort.

Adhesive Tape: Medical tape helps secure dressings or bandages.

Safety Pins: Bandages and dressings can be fastened using safety pins.

CPR Mask: A CPR mask or face shield can be included for rescue breaths during cardiopulmonary resuscitation (CPR).

Emergency Contact Number Info: Keep a list of emergency phone numbers in the first aid bag, including those for the local emergency services and poison control.

Kit Maintenance and Replenishment:

Regular Inspection: Beekeepers should periodically check their first aid supplies to ensure everything is in working order and hasn't expired.

Replenishment: Replace used or expired items promptly to maintain a fully stocked and up-to-date first aid kit.

Customization: Consider personalizing the first aid kit based on specific needs or any known medical conditions or allergies of the beekeeper or their team members.

Training and Knowledge:

Knowledge: Beekeepers need to know about the components of their first aid kit and how to use each safely.

First Aid Training: Beekeepers might benefit from training to improve their knowledge and abilities to provide emergency care.

For beekeepers, having an adequately stocked and maintained first aid kit is crucial. It makes it possible to administer first aid quickly and effectively, safeguarding the safety of beekeepers and others around them as they work with bees. Always seek expert help if you have a severe injury or medical emergency.

CHAPTER 4: GETTING STARTED WITH BEEKEEPING

Beekeeping is a crucial starting point for novices since it gives an overview of the essential components of beginning a beekeeping adventure. It covers critical subjects, including comprehending various bee species, choosing an appropriate place for your beehive, and accepting the necessary tools and equipment. A more thorough explanation of each section is provided below:

SECTION 1: UNDERSTANDING DIFFERENT TYPES OF BEES

You will learn more about the several bee species, including the honeybee species Apis mellifera, that are utilized in beekeeping in this region. It will become more apparent what the queen bee, worker bees, and drones are responsible for doing within a hive. Understanding the characteristics and behaviours of each type of bee can help you manage your colonies more effectively.

SECTION 2: SELECTING AN APPROPRIATE LOCATION FOR YOUR BEEHIVE:

The location of your beehive will affect both the health of your bees and the effectiveness of your beekeeping efforts. Using the data in this area, you may evaluate elements like wind direction, accessibility, and closeness to forage sources. Additionally, you'll learn how to address any problems and obstacles, such as neighbourhood anxieties or zoning rules.

SECTION 3: ESSENTIAL BEEKEEPING EQUIPMENT AND TOOLS:

For successful beekeeping and hive management, you need specialized equipment and instruments. You will learn about the necessary beekeeping tools in this section, including hive parts like the body, frames, and foundation. Additionally, you'll learn about safety equipment, smokers, beekeeping equipment, and other instruments required for inspections and regular maintenance. You may build a well-stocked beekeeping toolbox by comprehending the function and application of each piece of equipment.

You'll be ready to start beekeeping after finishing Chapter 4. You'll be knowledgeable about the principles of bee biology, able to assess and select the best location for your beehive, and equipped with the tools and resources required for efficient hive management. The foundation for this Chapter is laid by the other chapters, where you'll learn more about the challenges of beekeeping and how to manage your bee colonies.

CHAPTER 5: CHOOSING YOUR BEES

This Chapter addresses the critical issue of selecting bees for your beekeeping business. It overviews several bee species, subspecies, and considerations when choosing bees suited to your objectives and local circumstances. An overview of the important topics discussed in this Chapter is given below:

SECTION 1: BEE SPECIES AND SUBSPECIES

Learn about the many bee species and subspecies used in beekeeping in this section. The honeybee species Apis mellifera, which includes a multitude of subspecies with distinctive traits and adaptations to various settings and temperatures, is the main subject of this study. You'll learn about the characteristics, advantages, and potential drawbacks of subspecies such as Italian, Carniolan, and Buckfast Bees.

SECTION 2: FACTORS TO CONSIDER IN BEE SELECTION

The ideal bees for your beekeeping business should be chosen after considering various factors. Climate, local forage supply, disease resistance, production, behaviour, and adaptation are all covered in this section. You may select the bees best for your area and objectives by being aware of these aspects and analyzing your particular conditions.

SECTION 3: SOURCES FOR OBTAINING BEES

Once you've chosen the breed of bees you wish to keep, you must locate a reliable supplier. The many avenues for acquiring bees are examined in this section, including neighbourhood beekeepers, beekeeping supply shops, package bee providers, and nucleus colonies (nucs). You'll discover the benefits and factors of each provider and how to guarantee the well-being and calibre of the bees you buy.

SECTION 4: INTRODUCING BEES TO YOUR HIVE

After getting your bees, it's essential to acclimate them to their new hive properly. This Chapter provides instructions on introducing bees to their new population using package installation, nuc transfer, and queen introduction. You'll learn the significance of a gradual acclimatization technique to reduce stress and ensure the bees a comfortable transition.

You will have the information and considerations necessary to choose the bees for your beekeeping enterprise after reading Chapter 5. You may select bees appropriate for your objectives and surroundings by learning about various bee species and subspecies, evaluating variables like temperature and local circumstances, and investigating different sources for getting bees. You'll also learn how to correctly introduce your bees to their hive, preparing them for healthy colony formation and growth.

CHAPTER 6: BUILDING AND SETTING UP YOUR BEEHIVE

We are now talking about how to construct and set up your beehive. It covers essential subjects such as the variety of hives, how to assemble and prepare hive components, and where to situate the beehive for best results. A thorough description of each section is provided below:

SECTION 1: DIFFERENT TYPES OF HIVES: PROS AND CONS

In this part, you will learn about many types of hives typically used in beekeeping, including Langstroth, top bar, and Warre hives. This section analyses each hive type's characteristics, management concerns, and suitability for various beekeeping aims and preferences. Each hive type has benefits and drawbacks. Insights about hive accessibility, bee colony growth, honey output, and convenience of hive inspections will be shown, enabling you to select the kind of hive that best meets your requirements.

SECTION 2: ASSEMBLING AND PREPARING YOUR BEEHIVE COMPONENTS

This section walks you through putting the hive components together and getting them ready once you decide on your type. Making hive bodies, frames, foundations, inner covers, outer covers, and bottom boards correctly will be one of your newfound skills. The part also goes over essential factors like making sure there is enough ventilation inside the hive and that there is appropriate space between the frames. You can assemble a beehive that is structurally solid and functioning by following step-by-step directions and best practices.

SECTION 3: HOW TO POSITION YOUR BEEHIVE FOR BEST RESULTS:

The location of your beehive has a significant impact on the success of your beekeeping operation. In this section, you'll discover essential elements to consider while choosing where to set up your hive. Accessibility for hive inspections, wind direction, sun exposure, and nearby nectar and pollen sources are some of these factors. You'll also discover how to deal with problems like predator control and closeness to populated areas. If the hive's location is carefully selected and prepared, your bees will thrive and produce at their best.

Chapter 6 offers helpful guidance on building and assembling your beehive. By understanding the advantages and disadvantages of various hive types, correctly constructing hive components, and placing your hive in the optimum location, you can lay a solid foundation for beekeeping. This Chapter equips you with the skills and knowledge necessary to construct a suitable and functional hive for your bees, ensuring their comfort and well-being as they embark on their new journey.

CHAPTER 7: BEEKEEPING SAFETY AND BEST PRACTICES

Promoting excellent practices in beekeeping and ensuring beekeeper safety are the main goals of this section. It highlights the significance of taking safety precautions, treating bees properly, and implementing efficient management practices. Here is a thorough explanation of each team:

SECTION 1: BEEKEEPING SAFETY PRECAUTIONS

This section emphasizes the safety precautions beekeepers should take to lessen the risk of bee stings and other possible hazards. It is described how to ensure adequate physical protection by donning the appropriate protective clothing, such as a beekeeping suit, gloves, and a veil. It also highlights the value of being calm and self-assured while working with bees, being mindful of one's allergies, and having a backup plan in case of a mishap. A safe and happy beekeeping experience depends on knowing and using these safety measures.

SECTION 2: BEEHIVE INSPECTIONS AND MAINTENANCE

Regular hive inspections and maintenance are necessary for good beekeeping techniques. This section focuses on the best and safest ways to conduct hive inspections. It goes through subjects, including when to examine hives to cause the least disruption, how to gently handle frames to protect bees, and how to use a smoker to quiet bees down. It also provides instructions for controlling honey supers, maintaining and repairing hive components, and ensuring the hive has enough ventilation and is clean.

SECTION 3: BEE HEALTH AND DISEASE MANAGEMENT:

Maintaining the health of your bee colonies is essential for their long-term success. The ideal procedures for controlling and keeping track of bee health are covered in this section. It deals with problems, including recognizing the typical signs of insects and diseases that damage bees, taking precautions, and figuring out the best course of treatment. It also emphasizes the need for a balanced diet and provides several fodder options for your bees.

SECTION 4: SWARM MANAGEMENT

Honeybees swarm naturally, but effective management is required to avoid bee losses and preserve colony viability. The prevention and control of swarms are discussed in this section. It addresses issues such as identifying swarm preparations, managing strategies, and securely collecting and transporting hives.

SECTION 5: HONEY HARVESTING AND PROCESSING:

One of the most pleasurable parts of beekeeping is harvesting Honey. This section mainly emphasizes the best methods for gathering and processing honey. It covers the ideal time to extract Honey, how to eliminate honey supers, and the correct techniques for removing, filtering, and storing Honey. It also underlines the value of following hygienic standards while collecting and processing Honey.

Chapter 7 offers thorough guidance on beekeeping safety and best practices. By following the recommended safety precautions, using practical hive inspection and maintenance practices, controlling bee health and illnesses, practising swarm management, and guaranteeing correct honey harvesting and processing, beekeepers can provide a safe and productive environment for their bees. The importance of using ethical and informed beekeeping practices is emphasized in this Chapter since they support both the firm and the general health of the bees.

CHAPTER 8: THE BEEHIVE'S LIFECYCLE

In Chapter 8, the complicated lifecycle of a beehive is explored, along with the many stages and activities that a bee colony goes through as the seasons change. It gives a thorough explanation of the obligations bees have at different times of their lives. It emphasizes how important each stage is to the overall health and production of the hive. Here is a thorough explanation of the important topics discussed in this Chapter:

SECTION 1: THE BIRTH OF A BEE COLONY

This section examines how a new bee colony is started, beginning with entering a swarm or a package of bees into a hive. It talks about how combs are made, how brood is raised, and how the colony expands with the help of the queen bee. You'll learn more about the importance of nurse bees in raising the brood, worker bee development, and the progressive growth of the hive's population.

SECTION 2: ROLES AND RESPONSIBILITIES OF BEES

The sophisticated social structure of honeybees must be understood to appreciate the division of labour inside a bee colony fully. The functions of bees, including the queen bee, worker bees, and drones, are covered in this section. You'll learn about the queen's position in egg production, the worker bees' responsibilities in foraging, caring for the young, and maintaining the hive, and the drones' function in mating with the queen.

SECTION 3: SEASONAL ACTIVITIES OF THE HIVE

The hive's activities throughout the year are examined in this part, as well as how closely beekeeping is tied to the ebb and flow of the seasons. The spring buildup, when the hive population increases, the intense foraging and honey production during the summer, the preparations for winter survival, and the survival techniques used by the colony during the colder months are all covered in this article. You'll learn about the best times to do hive inspections, how to avoid swarms, and how to be ready for the winter and spring.

SECTION 4: REPRODUCTION AND SWARMING

This section examines the swarming phenomena and how honeybee colonies reproduce naturally. You'll discover the causes and warning signals of swarming, how queen cells are produced, how a new queen emerges, and how the swarm leaves the hive. The section also discusses swarm prevention and control techniques to maintain the hive population and production.

SECTION 5: HIVE DECLINE AND SUPERSEDURE

Bee colonies go through growth and decline cycles, and occasionally it's essential to replace a queen who is getting older or less effective. This section covers the phenomenon of supersedure, in which bees develop a new queen to replace an existing one. You'll learn about the symptoms of a failing queen, the supersedure procedure, and the significance of identifying and resolving queen problems to keep a hive healthy and productive.

The lifetime of a beehive is thoroughly explored in Chapter 8 to provide readers with a thorough grasp of the many phases and activities in a colony. Beekeepers may gain a greater understanding of the intricate and fascinating world of honeybees by understanding the formation of a bee colony, the duties and responsibilities of bees, the seasonal activities, reproduction and swarming, and the hive decline and supersedure process. This information is the basis for efficient hive management, enabling beekeepers to make wise choices and provide their colonies with the proper care throughout the year.

CHAPTER 9: BEEKEEPING TASKS THROUGHOUT THE YEAR

In the following section, the duties of year-round beekeeping are thoroughly discussed, emphasizing the seasonal issues and management techniques required to keep bee colonies healthy and productive. It outlines several obligations, and steps beekeepers should take to safeguard the health of their hives and boost honey production. Here is a thorough explanation of the important topics discussed in this Chapter:

SECTION 1: EARLY SPRING

The responsibilities and factors for early spring, a vital time for beekeepers, are discussed at the beginning of the Chapter. Examining the condition of the hive, feeding the bees as necessary, and keeping an eye out for symptoms of brood illnesses are all covered in this section. The significance of getting the hive ready for the approaching honey flow and solving overwintering problems are also covered.

SECTION 2: LATE SPRING AND SUMMER

Summertime brings a frenzy of activity for bees and beekeepers alike as the temperature increases and floral supplies become plentiful. This section focuses on managing pests and illnesses, preventing swarms, creating more room for honey storage, monitoring honey production, and preventing swarms. It also covers the significance of routine hive inspections to maintain the health and output of hives.

SECTION 3: FALL

This Chapter'sChapter highlights winter survival preparations when the season shifts towards October. Among the tasks is determining the hive's power and food supply.

I am applying treatments for varroa mites.

If required, supplement the feeding.

The pack is insulated to protect from lower temperatures.

The fall is an excellent time to prepare the hives for the winter and address any lingering issues.

SECTION 4: WINTER

The winter season is crucial for bee colonies. The tasks and considerations that must be considered for effective overwintering are the main topics of this section. It addresses issues including ensuring that the hive has enough air, preventing moisture buildup, keeping an eye on food supplies, and, if required, giving emergency feeding. In addition, methods for insulating hives and safeguarding against vermin-like mice are covered in this section.

SECTION 5: YEAR-ROUND TASKS

Beekeeping entails year-round duties that require care. The year-round activities covered in this part include record keeping, hive upkeep, equipment cleaning and storage, and continuous education. It emphasizes the need for lifelong learning and being up to date on beekeeping methods and research.

The significance of seasonal beekeeping chores and year-round management procedures is emphasized in Chapter 9. Beekeepers may successfully sustain the health of their colonies, avoid problems like swarming or colony collapse, and optimize honey output by comprehending and carrying out the activities indicated in each season. Regardless of the season, this Chapter acts as a helpful guide to make sure beekeepers are well-prepared and proactive in caring for their hives' bees.

CHAPTER 10: HARVESTING HONEY AND OTHER BEE PRODUCTS

Harvesting Honey and other essential bee products is the exciting and satisfying beekeeping component that is this section's subject. A thorough explanation of harvesting methods, tools, and factors is provided in this Chapter. It includes extracting Honey and producing other apiary goods such as royal jelly, propolis, and beeswax. Here is a breakdown of the major topics this Chapter covered:

SECTION 1: HONEY EXTRACTION

The process of extracting Honey marks the end of a productive beekeeping season. This section goes into detail on honey extraction from the hive. It covers subjects including removing honey supers, exposing the honeycomb cells, and extracting Honey using crush-and-strain or centrifugal processes. To ensure high-quality Honey, it also covers the significance of hygiene during the extraction process.

SECTION 2: HONEY FILTERING AND BOTTLING

The Honey must be filtered once extracted to eliminate contaminants and air bubbles. This section examines several filtering techniques to produce exact and pure Honey, such as fine mesh filters or gravity strainers. It also recommends appropriate bottling practices, such as sterilizing the containers, ensuring the airtight seals are intact, and labelling the jars with pertinent information.

SECTION 3: BEESWAX COLLECTION AND PROCESSING

This section focuses on the gathering and processing beeswax, a valuable substance acquired from bee colonies. It talks about gathering beeswax and cleaning it manually or with a solar wax melter. The course also discusses methods for removing impurities and converting beeswax to create candles and cosmetics, among other things.

SECTION 4: PROPOLIS COLLECTION AND UTILIZATION

This section investigates the gathering of propolis and its use. Bees gather propolis, a resinous substance. It discusses ways to collect propolis, including propolis screens or traps in the hive. It also emphasizes propolis's various applications, such as topical medicines, dental care products, and health supplements.

SECTION 5: ROYAL JELLY AND OTHER BEE PRODUCTS:

This section presents more bee products and summarises their collection and future use, including royal jelly and pollen. It goes through royal jelly's unique qualities, nutritional advantages, methods of extraction and storage and uses issues. The section also briefly discusses pollen collection techniques and their potential uses.

The contentment and benefits of collecting Honey and other bee products are emphasized in Chapter 10. Beekeepers may guarantee the production of premium honey by using the suggested methods for honey extraction, filtering, and bottling. The Chapter also offers information on how beeswax is gathered and processed.

CHAPTER 11 : EXPANDING YOUR BEEKEEPING KNOWLEDGE:

Chapter 11 encourages beekeepers to maintain developing their expertise in beekeeping. It emphasizes the need for lifelong learning, staying current on beekeeping method advancements, and exploring new hobbies. This Chapter thoroughly reviews many ways to increase your understanding of beekeeping. Here is a detailed summary of the important topics discussed in this Chapter:

SECTION 1: BEEKEEPING ASSOCIATIONS AND ORGANIZATIONS

The importance of joining regional beekeeping societies or organizations is emphasized in this section. It goes through the advantages of connecting with seasoned beekeepers, going to gatherings, workshops, and conferences, and taking part in training courses or mentorship possibilities. Associations for beekeepers offer helpful tools, encouragement, and chances to share expertise with other hobbyists.

SECTION 2: BOOKS AND PUBLICATIONS

Books and publications are crucial tools for increasing one's knowledge about beekeeping. The books, publications, and journals included in this area are excellent resources for learning about many facets of beekeeping. It discusses the value of creating a library for beekeeping information and offers suggestions for choosing reliable, current materials that appeal to various levels of competence and interests.

SECTION 3: ONLINE RESOURCES AND WEBSITES

The wealth of beekeeper-specific web resources is demonstrated in this section. The availability of information has altered significantly in the digital age. It encompasses reputable forums, websites, and online communities where beekeepers may engage in discussions, seek guidance, and exchange experiences. Thanks to internet technology, beekeepers may easily access a variety of beekeeping materials online and keep up with the most recent advancements in the industry.

SECTION 4: CONTINUING EDUCATION AND WORKSHOPS

Beekeeping is dynamic, making ongoing education crucial to staying current on new methods, scientific discoveries, and best practices. This section looks at possibilities for additional education, such as taking short beekeeping courses, seminars, and workshops. It highlights the need for practical training and hands-on learning opportunities where beekeepers may improve their abilities and obtain insightful knowledge from knowledgeable teachers.

SECTION 5: BEEKEEPING RESEARCH AND EXPERIMENTATION

This section explains the value of experimenting and the scientific method for beekeepers interested in trying out novel methods or performing research. To comprehend the distinctive dynamics of their bee colonies, it urges beekeepers to inspect their hives, maintain notes, and carry out small-scale experiments. It also emphasizes the opportunity to advance beekeeping knowledge by researching and disseminating results to a larger audience.

The necessity of ongoing research and education in beekeeping is emphasized in this Chapter. By participating in continuing education programs, joining beekeeping groups, building a library of beekeeping literature, accessing internet resources, and undertaking experiments and research, beekeepers may enhance their methods, increase their knowledge, and better understand beekeeping. This Chapter's goal is to serve as a reminder that learning about beekeeping is a lifelong endeavour and that the more work one puts into it, the more gratifying beekeeping will be.

CHAPTER 12: TROUBLESHOOTING COMMON BEEKEEPING CHALLENGES

This Chapter aims to arm beekeepers with the information and techniques they need to troubleshoot and solve typical problems that may arise during their beekeeping career. In-depth instructions are provided in this Chapter on how to recognize, avoid, and resolve any issues that beekeeping, or any other agricultural endeavour, may present. The following summarizes the key topics that were covered in this Chapter:

SECTION 1: IDENTIFYING HIVE HEALTH ISSUES

The significance of routinely checking and keeping an eye on hive health is emphasized in this section. It describes the typical warning signs and symptoms of hive health problems, including pests, infections, and difficulties relating to the queen, such as supersedure or queen failure, as well as brood diseases like American foulbrood and chalkbrood. It provides instructions for identifying these problems, running diagnostic tests, and applying the proper fixes.

SECTION 2: MANAGING VARROA MITES AND OTHER PESTS

One of the biggest threats to honeybee colonies, varroa mites, is the subject of this section's detection and management instructions. It covers numerous treatment alternatives, including chemical treatments, organic treatments, and integrated pest management strategies and describes various mite monitoring techniques, such as sugar roll or alcohol wash. The section offers advice on managing the populations of many common pests, including wax moths and tiny hive beetles.

SECTION 3: DEALING WITH HONEYBEE DISEASES

Several illnesses that influence the health of hives and honey production can impact beekeeping. This section discusses common honeybee diseases, including American foulbrood, European foulbrood, nosema, and chalkbrood, and how to identify, stop, and treat them. The necessity for proper hygiene, disease prevention, and early intervention is emphasized as the book explains the signs, modes of transmission and available treatments for various ailments.

SECTION 4: ADDRESSING QUEEN ISSUES

A productive bee colony depends on a healthy queen. Thus this section focuses on problems that frequently affect the queen's health. It examines indicators of a failing queen, such as a decline in brood production or the lack of eggs, and offers advice on identifying problems with the queen and putting the proper fixes in place. It includes replacing the queen, introducing a new queen, or letting the bees naturally raise their queen.

SECTION 5: ADDRESSING SEASONAL CHALLENGES

This section discusses the problems of various seasons and how they affect beekeeping. It covers topics including swarming, controlling the number of hives, supplementing nutrition amid nectar shortages, and preparing colonies for winter survival. It offers tactics and best practices for handling these periodic difficulties so colonies can stay wholesome and fruitful all year.

Chapter 12 provides beekeepers with the information and resources needed to address typical issues that could arise throughout their beekeeping endeavours. Beekeepers may successfully troubleshoot difficulties and protect the health of their colonies by recognizing hive health issues, controlling pests and illnesses, dealing with queen-related problems, and navigating seasonal hurdles. This Chapter gives beekeepers the tools they need to overcome challenges and keep their beekeeping businesses prospering.

CHAPTER 13: SUSTAINABLE BEEKEEPING PRACTICES

This Chapter emphasizes the significance of using sustainable beekeeping methods that provide a long-term emphasis on the health of bees, the environment, and beekeeping operations. Beekeepers can employ a range of sustainable techniques, explored in-depth in this Chapter, to lessen negative consequences and promote the sustainability of their beekeeping endeavours. Below is a detailed review of the crucial subjects covered in this Chapter:

SECTION 1: NATURAL BEEKEEPING METHODS

This section examines organic beekeeping practices that put the needs and behaviours of bees first. It covers methods including employing foundationless frames, letting bees create their comb, and building hives from raw materials. It highlights the importance of giving bees a natural, chemical-free habitat to support their health and well-being.

SECTION 2: INTEGRATED PEST MANAGEMENT (IPM)

IPM is an environmentally friendly method of controlling pests and illnesses. The IPM guiding principles and instructions for applying IPM tactics to beekeeping are highlighted in this section. It strongly emphasizes adopting non-chemical management strategies, including keeping track of mite levels, encouraging solid colonies, and using resistant bee stock. The responsible use of remedies when necessary is also covered, taking into account any possible adverse effects on bees and the environment.

SECTION 3: NATIVE PLANTS AND POLLINATOR-FRIENDLY LANDSCAPES

Supporting the foraging requirements of bees and other pollinators requires the creation of pollinator-friendly habitats. This section stresses the value of establishing native plants since they offer a varied and plentiful source of nectar and pollen all year. It directs the selection of plants that are appealing to bees, the creation of various habitats, and the reduction of pesticide usage close to beehives.

SECTION 4: CONSERVATION AND HABITAT PROTECTION

Sustainable beekeeping depends heavily on conservation and habitat protection. The significance of safeguarding bee-feeding regions, biodiversity, and natural ecosystems is covered in this section. To guarantee that bees have access to the proper feeding supplies, it considers techniques including habitat restoration, building bee-friendly corridors, and participating in conservation initiatives.

SECTION 5: RESPONSIBLE HIVE MANAGEMENT

Sustainable beekeeping requires responsible hive management. This section addresses dependable hive siting to reduce disturbance and increase feeding possibilities, suitable ventilation to prevent moisture accumulation and condensation, and appropriate swarm management to avoid the loss of priceless colonies. It also highlights the value of routine hive inspections, record-keeping, and continual education to enhance beekeeping techniques.

SECTION 6: BEEKEEPER EDUCATION AND OUTREACH

For the long-term success of the beekeeping community, education on sustainable beekeeping methods for both oneself and others is crucial. This section encourages beekeepers to participate in educational and outreach activities, including seminars, mentorship programs, and volunteer work in the community. It highlights the value of information sharing while advancing ethical beekeeping methods and bringing attention to bees' critical function in ecosystems.

Chapter 13 promotes using sustainable beekeeping techniques to guarantee the well-being of bees, protect the environment, and support the long-term financial success of beekeeping enterprises. By utilizing natural beekeeping methods, including pest management, creating pollinator-friendly landscapes, safeguarding habitats, and managing hives responsibly, beekeepers may create environmentally friendly and sustainable beekeeping enterprises. This Chapter guides beekeepers who desire to make a positive impact while benefiting from their line of work.

CONCLUSION:

The epilogue considers the beekeeper's experiences and accomplishments while encouraging others to take up beekeeping. By presenting intermediate and advanced beekeeping skills, it also looks ahead to the future. An explanation of each subsection of the conclusion chapter is provided below:

SECTION 1: REFLECTING ON YOUR BEEKEEPING JOURNEY AND ACHIEVEMENTS

The beekeeper is urged to reflect on their experience as beginning beekeepers and their successes in this part. The reader is inspired to reflect on the difficulties they have faced, the insights they have gained, and the joy beekeeping has brought them. Through this reflection, the beekeeper may recognize their advancement and positive effects on their colonies and the environment.

SECTION 2: INSPIRING OTHERS TO GET INVOLVED IN BEEKEEPING

This section encourages readers to begin beekeeping since it is a lovely and pleasurable hobby. It calls attention to the benefits of beekeeping, such as preserving pollinators, producing delicious Honey, and forging closer ties with the natural world. The section highlights the significance of sharing information, skills, and passion with others to inspire and support starting beekeepers.

SECTION 3: LOOKING AHEAD: INTERMEDIATE AND ADVANCED BEEKEEPING TECHNIQUES

This section gives a glimpse into the beekeeper's future by outlining advanced and intermediate techniques. It acknowledges that beekeepers may be willing to research progressively complicated beekeeping issues as they gain confidence and skill. Queen raising, honeybee genetics, hive splitting, and specialized honey production methods are all briefly discussed. It highlights the significance of beekeeping's ongoing learning and development.

The last Chapter offers a thoughtful conclusion to the beginner's introduction to beekeeping, challenging the reader to reflect on their achievements, inspire others to join the beekeeping community, and consider expanding their study and training. It supports the idea that beekeeping is a career that offers numerous opportunities for growth, education, and a good influence on the environment and the bee community.